D0581720

Buitoni

THE BUITONI PASTA COOKBOOK

Colour Library Books

INTRODUCTION

Pasta has been an Italian national dish for more than four centuries. Its popularity is such that it is now a vital part of the typical Italian diet, providing essential protein and carbohydrate, with only minimal fat.

The history of pasta can be traced back to the ancient Greeks and Romans who made a mixture of flour and water, cut it into thin strips and cooked it. There were even remains of basic pasta making equipment found in the ruins of Pompeii.

The history of **Buitoni** pasta began in 1827 in the small Tuscan town of Sansepolcro where Giulia Buitoni and her husband Giovanni set up the world's first dry pasta making plant with only a handful of workers and primitive machinery. Today, the **Buitoni** brand is known around the world for a range of top quality Italian foods including sauces, tomato purée, Grissini sticks, Parmesan cheese, ravioli, olive oil, chilled meats, frozen foods and rice, as well as pasta. Such are the qualities of **Buitoni's** extensive range of dried pasta that it remains the company's biggest seller.

Buitoni pasta comes in many shapes and sizes, each shape being specially made for a particular sauce. Long pasta such as spaghetti is best with a light sauce, flat strips of pasta such as fettuccine are delicious with a heavier sauce, whilst tubular pasta is generally used in baked dishes. Real Italian pasta, such as **Buitoni**, is always made with durum wheat, which is milled into semolina with water and sometimes with egg. Spinach, tomato and other ingredients can also be added to give colour. A splendid example of this is Eliche Tricolore with its spirals of red, yellow and green pasta representing the Italian flag.

Pasta consumption is booming around the world, particularly in Britain, where more and more people are appreciating the versatility and nutritional value of pasta, although we have a long way to go before we catch up with the Southern Italians who eat, on average, 40 kilograms of pasta a year!

For sheer versatility and ease of cooking, nothing surpasses pasta, and the recipes in this book provide all the inspiration to enjoy different kinds of pasta in both simple and creative dishes. With **Buitoni**, everyone can share the Italian love of food.

CLB 2687

Printed in Singapore.

ISBN 0 86283 868 1

Buitoni
Fettuccine
Cottura: 6 min.
Buitoni
Farfalle
Cottura: 9 min.
Buitoni
CANNELLONI
Buitoni
Lasagne
Cottura: 11 min.
Pasta di semola di grano duro
con pomodoro e spinaci
ONDULI
CHIOCCI
DALLA CASA BUITONI

Buitoni®

LASAGNE CON VEGETALI

(Vegetable Lasagne)
SERVES 4-6

This brightly coloured lasagne is perfect for a special family meal or an informal dinner party.

15ml/1 tbsp olive oil
2 onions, finely chopped
2 red peppers, deseeded and chopped
2 green peppers, deseeded and chopped
425g/15oz can chopped tomatoes
1 clove garlic, crushed
60ml/4 tbsps **Buitoni** tomato purée
10ml/2 tsps fresh basil, chopped
Salt and freshly ground black pepper
20g/¾oz butter
20g/¾oz flour
285ml/½ pint milk
75g/3oz Gruyère cheese, grated
9 sheets **Buitoni** Lasagne Verdi

1. Preheat oven to 180°C/350°F/Gas Mark 4.

2. Heat the oil in a large frying pan and fry the onions and peppers for 4-5 minutes until softened, then add the tomatoes, garlic, tomato purée, basil and seasoning. Cover and simmer for 30 minutes.

STEP 2

3. Meanwhile, melt the butter, add the flour, and cook for 1-2 minutes, stirring continuously. Remove from the heat and gradually stir in the milk.

STEP 3

4. Return to the heat and cook, stirring until the sauce is thickened and smooth. Add half the cheese and season well.

5. Spoon a little of the pepper sauce into a 28x17cm/11x7-inch rectangular ovenproof dish and add a layer of lasagne, without overlapping. Continue with alternate layers of lasagne and pepper sauce, finishing with a layer of lasagne.

STEP 5

6. Spread the cheese sauce over the top and sprinkle with the remaining grated cheese. Bake for 25-30 minutes.

Cook's Notes

TIME: Preparation takes 10 minutes, cooking takes about 70 minutes.

SERVING IDEA: Serve with a salad of crisp lettuce, spring onions, celery, chopped apple and walnut pieces.

COOK'S TIP: Do not attempt to add the milk to the butter and flour mixture whilst it is still on the heat, as the mixture will become lumpy.

CANNELLONI CON SPINACI E MANDORLE

(Spinach and Almond Cannelloni)

SERVES 6

This unusual meat-free dish is good enough to serve on any occasion.

Filling

350g/12oz fresh spinach
30ml/2 tbsps olive oil
1 large onion, finely chopped
1 clove garlic, crushed
1 green pepper, deseeded and finely chopped
50g/2oz ground almonds
25g/1oz whole almonds, finely chopped
20ml/4 tsps fresh oregano, chopped
140ml/¼ pint vegetable stock
2.5ml/½ tsp nutmeg
Salt and freshly ground pepper

12 **Buitoni** Cannelloni tubes

Sauce

1 medium onion, finely chopped
425g/15oz can chopped tomatoes
5ml/1 tsp sugar
75g/3oz Mozzarella cheese, sliced

1. Preheat oven to 200°C/400°F/Gas Mark 6.

2. Blanch the spinach in boiling water for 1 minute. Drain well and chop finely.

3. Heat 15ml/1 tbsp of the oil in a large saucepan and fry the onion, garlic and pepper for 3-4 minutes until soft. Add the spinach, almonds, 10ml/2 tsps of the oregano, stock, nutmeg and seasoning. Cook for a further 2-3 minutes.

STEP 2

4. Fill the cannelloni with the spinach mixture and place them in a lightly greased, shallow ovenproof dish.

STEP 4

5. Heat the remaining oil in a large saucepan and fry the onion for 4-5 minutes until browned. Add the tomato, remaining oregano and sugar and bring to the boil. Cook for 5 minutes.

6. Pour the sauce over the cannelloni, top with the Mozzarella and bake for 30-35 minutes. Serve immediately.

Cook's Notes

TIME: Preparation takes 30 minutes, cooking takes 30-35 minutes.

SERVING IDEA: Serve this filling dish with a fresh green salad, lightened by the addition of chopped green apple.

VARIATION: Substitute chopped, cooked broccoli for the spinach.

COOK'S TIP: If you find it difficult to fill the cannelloni tubes, use a piping bag to pipe the spinach mixture into the tubes.

INSALATA DI POLLO E CARCIOFI

(Chicken and Artichoke Salad)
SERVES 4

A delightfully different meal which is perfect for summer entertaining.

Dressing
90ml/6 tbsps olive oil
30ml/2 tbsps wine vinegar
2 cloves garlic, crushed
10ml/2 tsps French mustard
30ml/2 tbsps fresh parsley, chopped

150g/6oz **Buitoni** Eliche
150g/6oz cooked chicken, chopped
1 can artichoke hearts, roughly chopped

1. Place all the dressing ingredients in a screw top jar and shake thoroughly.

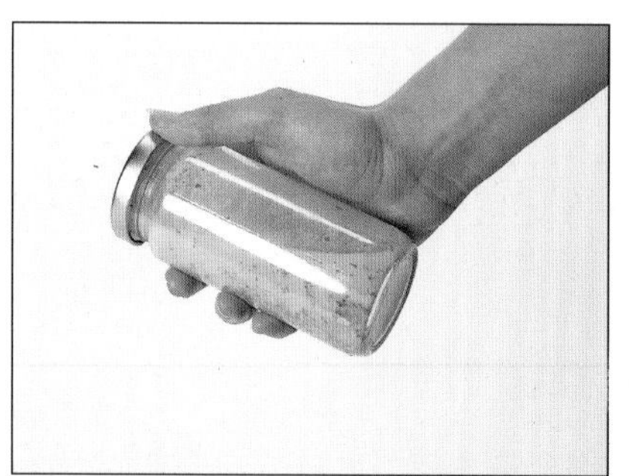

STEP 1

2. Cook the pasta as directed on the packet, drain and place in a serving dish. Whilst the pasta is still warm, pour over the dressing and mix well. Allow pasta to cool thoroughly.

STEP 2

3. Stir in the chicken and artichokes and season to taste.

STEP 3

Cook's Notes

TIME: Preparation takes 30 minutes.

SERVING IDEA: Add some seedless green grapes to the pasta salad.

VARIATION: Use wholegrain mustard instead of the French mustard.

COOK'S TIP: Always make sure the chicken is completely cooked before using.

FETTUCCINE ALLA GENOVESE

(Fettuccine in Pesto Sauce)
SERVES 4

This adaptable dish can be served in smaller quantities as a starter.

340g/12oz **Buitoni** Fettuccine
4 fresh basil leaves, wiped clean
2 cloves garlic, peeled
75g/3oz pine nuts
125ml/4½ fl oz extra virgin olive oil
60g/2½oz freshly grated Parmesan cheese
Salt and freshly ground black pepper
Chopped basil for garnish

1. Cook the pasta as directed on the packet.

2. Chop the basil leaves and garlic.

3. In a pestle, grind the garlic to a paste and add the basil leaves. Pound until the leaves begin to break up.

STEP 3

4. Add the nuts and pound to a paste, dribble the oil slowly into the paste and pound until it is all incorporated.

STEP 4

5. Transfer to a bowl, add the cheese and stir until evenly blended.

STEP 5

6. Add 2 tbsps of the cooking water to the prepared sauce and season to taste. Stir, then toss through the drained pasta. Sprinkle with chopped basil before serving.

Cook's Notes

TIME: Preparation takes 10 minutes, cooking takes 20-25 minutes.

COOK'S TIP: If you have a food processor, place all the ingredients except the pasta in the machine and blend until it becomes a rough textured sauce, then toss through the pasta as above.

GNOCCHI CON SALSA DI NOCI

(Gnocchi in a walnut sauce)
SERVES 4

This attractive dish is suitable for any occasion and is also perfect fare for a meat-free meal.

225g/8oz **Buitoni** Gnocchi
15g/½oz walnut pieces
50g/2oz toasted pine nuts
50g/2oz butter
15ml/1 tbsp olive oil
1 clove garlic, crushed
100g/4oz Ricotta cheese
Salt and freshly ground pepper
25g/1oz freshly grated Parmesan cheese
Chervil sprigs for garnish

1. Cook the pasta as directed on the packet.

2. Meanwhile, place the walnuts, 40g/1½oz of the pine nuts, butter, oil and garlic in a food processor. Blend until smooth.

STEP 2

3. Add the Ricotta and seasoning and mix well.

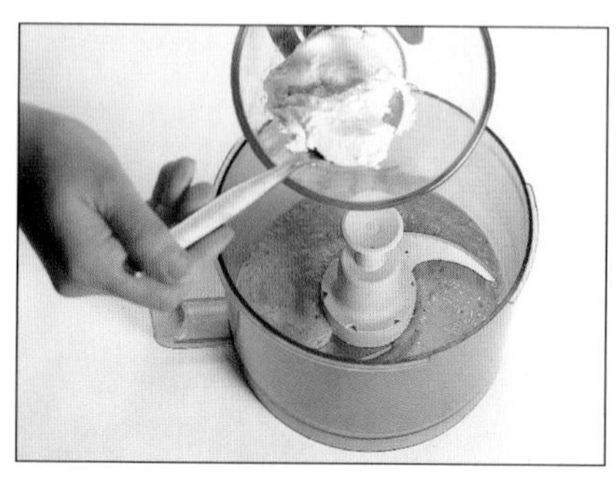

STEP 3

4. Drain the pasta, toss in the sauce and serve sprinkled with Parmesan cheese.

STEP 4

5. Garnish with chervil sprigs and the remaining pine nuts, and serve immediately.

Cook's Notes

TIME: Preparation takes 5 minutes, cooking takes 20-25 minutes.

SERVING IDEA: Serve with chunks of bread which have been rubbed with garlic, toasted, covered with fresh tomatoes, seasoned and drizzled with olive oil.

VARIATION: Substitute any of the many other pasta shapes in the **Buitoni** range for the gnocchi.

COOK'S TIP: If a food processor is not available, chop the nuts by hand.

FETTUCCINE ALLA PESCATORA

(Prawn and Clam Fettuccine)
SERVES 4-6

This delicious dish is perfect for informal entertaining.

350g/12oz **Buitoni** Fettuccine Verdi
25g/1oz butter
1 onion, chopped
30ml/2 tbsps plain flour
55ml/2 fl oz fish stock
410g/14½oz can Carnation evaporated milk
275g/10oz can baby clams, drained
150g/6oz peeled prawns, defrosted if frozen
Rind of 1 lemon, grated
15ml/1 tbsp lemon juice
Freshly chopped parsley to garnish

1. Cook the pasta as directed on the packet.

2. Melt the butter in a saucepan and gently fry the onion until soft. Stir in the flour.

STEP 2

3. Gradually blend in the fish stock and evaporated milk and simmer for 2 minutes.

STEP 3

4. Stir in the clams, prawns, lemon rind and juice. Heat thoroughly and toss with the freshly cooked fettuccine. Serve garnished with parsley.

STEP 4

Cook's Notes

TIME: Preparation takes 5 minutes, cooking takes 15 minutes.

SERVING IDEA: Serve with broccoli and cooked baby tomatoes.

VARIATION: Substitute any shellfish such as mussels, scallops etc. for the clams.

COOK'S TIP: To make fish stock, simmer uncooked fish bones in water with a slice of onion and mixed herbs for 30 minutes, then cool completely before using.

RAVIOLI AL BURRO

(Buttered Ravioli)
SERVES 4

This tasty dish is easy to prepare and is the perfect mid-week meal.

250g/9oz **Buitoni** Ravioli
75g/3oz butter
1 clove garlic, crushed
10-12 fresh sage leaves, chopped
2.5ml/½ tsp nutmeg
Salt and freshly ground pepper
25g/1oz freshly grated Parmesan cheese
Chopped parsley for garnish

1. Cook the ravioli as directed on the packet.

STEP 1

2. Melt the butter in a small saucepan, add the garlic, sage, nutmeg, and seasoning and fry for 1-2 minutes.

STEP 2

3. Drain the ravioli and toss with the butter mixture and 15g/½oz of the Parmesan.

STEP 3

4. Serve sprinkled with the remaining Parmesan and the chopped parsley.

TIME: Preparation takes 5 minutes, cooking takes 15 minutes.

SERVING IDEA: Serve with slices of fresh crusty bread drizzled with extra virgin olive oil and toasted until golden brown.

VARIATION: Stir in a tablespoon of chopped almonds when frying the garlic mixture.

COOK'S TIP: **Buitoni** Ravioli is a useful standby to have in the kitchen as it keeps for a year.

MADE IN SWEDEN

PENNE RIGATE AL FORNO

(Baked Pasta Quills)
SERVES 4

A substantial, hearty pasta dish suitable for big appetites or a cold night when the family needs a good meal.

125g/5oz minced beef
75g/3oz freshly grated Parmesan cheese
25g/1oz freshly made breadcrumbs
1 egg, beaten
15ml/1 tbsp fresh parsley, chopped
1 clove garlic, crushed
Salt and freshly ground black pepper
45ml/3 tbsps olive oil
200ml/7 fl oz red wine
125g/5oz cooked spicy sausage, sliced
400g/14oz can Italian chopped tomatoes
125g/5oz **Buitoni** Penne Rigate
3 hard-boiled eggs, sliced
150g/6oz Mozzarella cheese

1. Preheat oven to 200°C/400°F/Gas Mark 6.

2. Mix together the beef, one third of the Parmesan, breadcrumbs, egg, parsley, garlic and seasoning to taste, until thoroughly blended. Shape into 20 small balls.

3. Gently fry the meatballs in oil for 5 minutes, then add the wine and cook until evaporated. Stir in the sausage and tomatoes and simmer for 20 minutes.

4. Cook the pasta as directed on the packet, and drain.

STEP 2

5. Pour a layer of tomato sauce into the base of the ovenproof dish. Then build up alternate layers of pasta, Parmesan, egg, sliced Mozzarella and sauce, finishing with a layer of sauce, and finally some Parmesan.

STEP 5

6. Cover with foil and bake in the preheated oven for 15-20 minutes or until the cheese has melted.

Cook's Notes

TIME: Preparation takes 30 minutes, cooking takes 45-50 minutes.

VARIATION: Replace the minced beef with minced lamb.

SERVING IDEA: Serve with a freshly made coleslaw salad.

COOK'S TIP: Chill the meatballs prior to cooking as this helps them keep their shape.

FARFALLE ALLA RUSSA

(Pasta Bows with Smoked Salmon Sauce)
SERVES 4 as a starter

A delicate, pretty dish suitable for a dinner party or an indulgent meal!

225g/8oz **Buitoni** Farfalle
12g/½oz butter
100g/4oz button mushrooms, halved
285ml/½ pint single cream
150g/6oz smoked salmon, cut into strips
30ml/2 tbsps grappa liqueur or vodka
Freshly ground pepper
Fresh tarragon to garnish

1. Cook the pasta as directed on the packet.

2. Meanwhile, melt the butter in a large frying pan, add the mushrooms and cook for 4-5 minutes until just browned.

STEP 2

3. Gradually add the cream, salmon and grappa or vodka, and cook for 1-2 minutes until heated through. Season with pepper.

STEP 3

4. Drain the pasta and toss in the cream sauce. Sprinkle with the fresh tarragon before serving.

STEP 4

Cook's Notes

TIME: Preparation takes 5 minutes, cooking takes 20 minutes.

SERVING IDEA: Serve with a salad of Frisée lettuce and halved seedless green grapes.

VARIATION: Substitute smoked salmon trout for the salmon.

COOK'S TIP: Do not use canned salmon as this will spoil the taste of the dish.

FARFALLE ALLA CACCIATORA

(Pasta Bows with Pork and Red Wine)
SERVES 4

The sauce in this delicious recipe is quite thin and full flavoured from the red wine, herbs and meat juices.

15ml/1 tbsp olive oil
2 cloves garlic, crushed
350g/12oz pork fillet, sliced into rounds
15ml/1 tbsp capers
15ml/1 tbsp fresh sage leaves, chopped
5ml/1 tsp fresh rosemary leaves, chopped
285ml/½ pint red wine
Salt and freshly ground black pepper
225g/8oz **Buitoni** Farfalle
Rosemary sprigs to garnish

1. Heat the olive oil in a large pan and fry the garlic and pork for 5-8 minutes until golden. Add the capers, sage and rosemary and cook for a further 2-3 minutes.

STEP 1

2. Add the wine and bring to the boil. Simmer for 10-15 minutes until the pork is cooked through and the wine is reduced. Season to taste.

STEP 2

3. Cook the pasta in salted boiling water as directed on the packet and toss in the red wine sauce. Serve immediately garnished with extra rosemary sprigs.

STEP 3

Cook's Notes

TIME: Preparation takes 10 minutes, cooking takes 25-30 minutes.

SERVING IDEAS: Serve with a chicory and orange salad.

VARIATION: Lamb fillet is delicious in place of the pork.

COOK'S TIP: If capers are unavailable, use 15g/1 tbsp of chopped gherkins.

SPAGHETTI CON SUGO DI FEGATO

(Spaghetti with Liver Sauce)
SERVES 4

A quick and easy-to-prepare dish – perfect for lunch or supper.

Sauce
140ml/¼ pint water
450g/1lb calves' or pigs' liver, washed and sliced
100g/4oz bacon, cut into small pieces
400g/14oz can Italian peeled tomatoes
225g/8oz mushrooms, washed and sliced
1 garlic clove, crushed
5ml/1 tsp mixed herbs

30g/1oz butter
30g/1oz flour
350g/12oz **Buitoni** Spaghetti
Chopped parsley to garnish

Slicing liver

1. Preheat oven to 190°C/375°F/Gas Mark 5.

2. Put all ingredients for the sauce into a casserole dish. Stir and cover. Bake in the oven for 45 minutes, stirring occasionally.

STEP 2

3. Cook the pasta as directed on the packet. Drain, and place in a hot serving dish.

STEP 3

4. Blend the butter and flour together and stir bit-by-bit into the liver casserole juices and heat until thickened.

5. Pour the hot sauce over the pasta and serve sprinkled with the chopped parsley.

Cook's Notes

TIME: Preparation takes 10-15 minutes, cooking takes 45 minutes.

SERVING IDEA: Serve with green beans tossed in melted butter and garlic.

VARIATION: Fry onion rings and streaky bacon until golden brown and crispy and sprinkle over the dish before serving.

CELLENTANI AL POMODORO CON FUNGHI E PROSCIUTTO

(Pasta Whirls with Tomato, Mushroom and Ham Sauce)
SERVES 4

This delicious, brightly coloured pasta dish has a rich buttery flavour.

300g/10oz **Buitoni** Cellentani
100g/4oz button mushrooms, sliced
2 cloves garlic, crushed
75g/3oz butter
100g/4oz cooked peas
100g/4oz cooked ham, chopped
4 tomatoes, peeled and chopped
60ml/4 tbsps double cream or crème fraîche
Salt and freshly ground pepper
Parmesan cheese to serve

1. Cook the pasta as directed on the packet.

2. Meanwhile, cook mushrooms and garlic in butter until tender. Add peas, ham and tomatoes and cook for a further 2-3 minutes. Season to taste.

STEP 2

STEP 2

3. Drain the cooked pasta and place in a warm serving bowl.

4. Stir in the sauce, cream and seasoning. Serve immediately, accompanied by the Parmesan cheese.

STEP 4

Cook's Notes

TIME: Preparation takes 5 minutes, cooking takes 15-20 minutes.

SERVING IDEAS: Serve with garlic bread and a mixed salad.

VARIATION: For a vegetarian meal substitute 50g/2oz cap mushrooms and 50g/2oz oyster mushrooms for the ham. Slice the mushrooms thinly and add with the garlic.

PENNE ALL' AMATRICIANA

(Pasta Quills in a Tomato and Bacon Sauce)

SERVES 4

A quick and tasty pasta dish which is sure to be a hit with children.

15ml/1 tbsp olive oil
1 medium onion, sliced into rings
100g/4oz back bacon, chopped
140ml/¼ pint dry white wine
425g/15oz can Italian chopped tomatoes
Salt and freshly ground pepper
5ml/1 tsp fresh basil, roughly chopped
350g/12oz **Buitoni** Penne Rigate
75g/3oz freshly grated Parmesan cheese
Basil sprigs to garnish

1. Heat the oil in a large pan and fry the onion for 3-4 minutes until translucent. Add the bacon and cook for a further 3-4 minutes. Add the wine, tomatoes, seasoning and basil.

STEP 1

2. Bring to the boil and simmer for 10-15 minutes until reduced.

3. Meanwhile, cook the pasta as directed on the packet.

4. Drain well, toss in the hot sauce and serve immediately sprinkled with Parmesan cheese and basil sprigs.

STEP 1

STEP 4

Cook's Notes

TIME: Preparation takes 5 minutes, cooking takes 15-20 minutes.

SERVING IDEA: Serve with sliced tomatoes and shredded spring onions drizzled with extra virgin olive oil.

VARIATION: For a touch of extra flavour, substitute red onion and smoked bacon for the onion and back bacon.

COOK'S TIP: The easiest way to slice an onion into rings is to hold the onion steady with a fork whilst you slice.

GNOCCHI AI QUATTRO FORMAGGI

(Gnocchi with Four Cheeses)
SERVES 4

Cheese fans will love this extravaganza of some of Italy's best loved produce, enhanced with breadcrumbs and pasta.

225g/8oz **Buitoni** Gnocchi
50g/2oz butter
50g/2oz flour
550ml/1 pint milk
25g/1oz Gruyère cheese, grated
25g/1oz Mozzarella cheese, sliced
120g/4oz Dolcelatte cheese, diced
60ml/4 tbsps freshly grated Parmesan cheese
Salt and freshly ground black pepper
15ml/1 tbsp wholemeal breadcrumbs, toasted
Chopped chives to garnish

1. Cook the pasta as directed on the packet.

2. Meanwhile, melt the butter in a large pan. Stir in the flour and cook for 1-2 minutes, stirring continuously. Remove from the heat and gradually stir in the milk.

STEP 2

3. Return to the heat and cook, stirring until the sauce has thickened. Stir in the cheeses and cook gently for 2-3 minutes until melted. Season to taste.

STEP 3

4. Drain the pasta and toss in the hot sauce. Serve immediately sprinkled with the breadcrumbs and chives.

STEP 4

Cook's Notes

TIME: Preparation takes 15 minutes, cooking takes 15-20 minutes.

SERVING IDEA: Serve with a mixture of radicchio, lamb's lettuce and Frisée, and crusty bread to mop up all the lovely sauce.

GRUYERE

TORTIGLIONI ALLA CARRETTIERA

(Tortiglioni with Parsley and Breadcrumbs)
SERVES 4

Crispy-fried breadcrumbs make this dish surprisingly tasty and the perfect fare for lunch or supper.

350g/12oz **Buitoni** Tortiglioni
75ml/5 tbsps olive oil
2 cloves garlic, crushed
1 small onion, finely chopped
25g/1oz fresh parsley, chopped
5ml/1 tsp fresh oregano, chopped
Salt and freshly ground pepper
25g/1oz butter
50g/2oz fresh, wholemeal breadcrumbs

1. Cook the pasta as directed on the packet.

2. Heat 45ml/3 tbsps of the oil in a frying pan and fry the garlic, onion and parsley for 3-4 minutes until softened. Add the oregano, drained pasta and seasoning, and mix well.

STEP 2

3. Heat the remaining oil and butter in another frying pan. Sauté the breadcrumbs until golden and crisp and add to the pasta. Toss well and serve immediately.

STEP 2

STEP 3

Cook's Notes

TIME: Preparation takes 10 minutes, cooking takes 15-20 minutes.

SERVING IDEA: Serve with a mixed salad.

VARIATION: For meat lovers, fry 2 chopped rashers of smoked back bacon with the garlic and onion mixture.

FETTUCCINE VERDI CON SALSA DI GRANCHIO

(Fettuccine Verdi with Crab Sauce)

SERVES 4

This delicate, pale coloured dish has the light and subtle flavour perfect for starters.

250g/9oz **Buitoni** Fettuccine Verdi
25g/1oz butter
225ml/8 fl oz single cream
170g/5½oz can crab meat in brine, drained
10ml/2 tsps vodka
Salt and freshly ground pepper
Lemon slices and dill to garnish

1. Cook the pasta as directed on the packet.

STEP 1

2. Meanwhile, melt the butter in a saucepan.

STEP 2

3. Add the remaining ingredients and simmer gently for 5 minutes.

STEP 3

4. Drain the pasta, place in a warm serving dish and mix in the hot sauce. Garnish with lemon slices and dill before serving.

Cook's Notes

TIME: Cooking takes 15-20 minutes.

SERVING IDEAS: Serve with sliced beefsteak tomatoes and a sprinkling of shredded basil to garnish.

VARIATION: If you like gin, use this instead of the vodka – the taste is just as delicious.

PIPE RIGATE AL POMODORO CON MOZZARELLA E OLIVE

(Pasta Pipes with Tomatoes, Mozzarella and Olives)
SERVES 4-6

Black olives and capers bring out all the flavour of this authentic Italian dish.

425g/15oz can Italian chopped tomatoes
1 clove garlic, crushed
5 fresh basil leaves, shredded
Salt and freshly ground pepper
400g/14oz **Buitoni** Pipe Rigate
30ml/2 tbsps olive oil
100g/4oz Mozzarella cheese, cut into thin strips
12 black olives, pitted and halved
30ml/2 tbsps capers, drained
15ml/1 tbsp oregano

Shredding basil

1. Place the tomatoes, garlic, basil and seasoning to taste, in a saucepan and simmer gently for 15 minutes.

STEP 1

2. Meanwhile, cook the pasta as directed on the packet. Drain the pasta and place in a warm serving dish.

3. Stir the remaining ingredients into the sauce and mix well. Toss the pasta in the sauce and serve immediately.

STEP 3

Cook's Notes

TIME: Preparation takes 10 minutes, cooking takes 15 minutes.

VARIATION: Add 50g/2oz walnut halves when adding the final ingredients.

COOK'S TIP: Shred the basil by placing the fresh leaves on top of each other, then fold them in half and slice finely.

CELLENTANI ALLA MARINARA

(Pasta Whirls with Seafood Sauce)
SERVES 4

This highly flavoured pasta dish is suitable for any occasion.

25g/1oz butter
1 small onion, finely chopped
25g/1oz flour
285ml/½ pint milk
140ml/¼ pint dry white wine
450g/1lb monkfish or cod fillet, cut into cubes
150g/6oz peeled prawns
Salt and freshly ground black pepper
225g/8oz **Buitoni** Cellentani
15ml/1 tbsp fresh dill, chopped

1. Melt the butter in a saucepan, add the onion and cook for 2-3 minutes. Stir in the flour and cook for a further 2 minutes.

STEP 1

2. Remove from the heat and gradually add the milk. Return to the heat and cook for 3-4 minutes, stirring continuously.

STEP 2

3. Gradually add the white wine and then the monkfish, prawns and seasoning. Simmer gently, stirring occasionally, for about 5 minutes, until the fish is cooked.

STEP 3

4. Meanwhile, cook the pasta according to the pack instructions. Drain and toss with the fish sauce. Sprinkle with the chopped dill and serve immediately.

Cook's Notes

TIME: Preparation takes 5 minutes, cooking takes 15-20 minutes.

SERVING IDEAS: Serve with a selection of young vegetables.

VARIATION: Use any white fish of your choice.

COOK'S TIP: Monkfish stays firm in texture once cooked, so is useful in numerous dishes.

MINESTRONE CON CONCHIGLIE

(Minestrone with Pasta Shells)
SERVES 4

A deliciously flavoured, hearty soup full of pasta shapes and a variety of vegetables.

120ml/8 tbsps pure olive oil
1 medium onion, chopped
25g/1oz bacon, minced
400g/14oz potatoes, peeled and diced
250g/9oz courgettes, diced
250g/9oz ripe tomatoes, diced
125g/5oz carrots, diced
75g/3oz leeks, sliced
1 celery heart, sliced
120g/4oz green beans, sliced
Salt
120g/4oz **Buitoni** Conchiglie
Pepper
30g/2 tbsps freshly grated Parmesan cheese

1. Heat half the oil in a large pan and sauté the onion and bacon.

STEP 1

2. Add the vegetables. Cover with 2 ltrs/3½ pints of boiling water, season with salt and cook for about 25 minutes.

STEP 2

3. Add the pasta, do not cover the pan, and cook for 15 minutes or until cooked.

STEP 3

4. Remove from heat and add pepper, Parmesan cheese and the remaining olive oil.

5. Allow to cool slightly, then transfer to soup bowls and serve.

Cook's Notes

TIME: Preparation takes 15-20 minutes, cooking takes 40 minutes.

SERVING IDEA: Serve with chunks of freshly baked crusty bread.

COOK'S TIP: It is not necessary to peel the potatoes and carrots if you like the skins, simply scrub them instead. This soup will freeze well if you freeze it before adding the cheese.

TORTELLINI CON PANNA E FUNGHI

(Tortellini with Cream and Mushrooms)

SERVES 4

A quick and easy dish to prepare, perfect for entertaining those unexpected guests.

250g/9oz **Buitoni** Tortellini
25g/1oz butter
1 medium red onion, sliced
150g/6oz button mushrooms, halved
285ml/10 fl oz single cream
Salt and freshly ground pepper
15ml/1 tbsp fresh parsley, chopped

1. Cook the tortellini as directed on the packet.

2. Meanwhile, melt the butter in a large frying pan and cook the onion for 5 minutes until golden brown.

STEP 2

3. Add the mushrooms and cook for a further 2-3 minutes. Add the cream, season and cook for 1-2 minutes until heated through.

STEP 3

4. Drain the pasta and toss in the cream sauce. Sprinkle with parsley and serve immediately.

STEP 4

Cook's Notes

TIME: Preparation takes 5 minutes, cooking takes 15-20 minutes.

SERVING IDEA: Serve with crusty rolls or garlic bread.

VARIATION: Add 100g/4oz chopped walnuts or almonds that have been toasted.

SPAGHETTI ALLA PUTTANESCA

(Spaghetti with Anchovies, Tomatoes, Olives and Capers)

SERVES 4

An everyday family meal which is both tasty and filling.

400g/14oz **Buitoni** Spaghetti
25g/1oz butter
2 cloves garlic, crushed
8 anchovy fillets, chopped
2.5cm/1-inch piece fresh chilli, seeded and finely chopped
400g/14oz can peeled and chopped Italian tomatoes
100g/4oz black olives, pitted and sliced
15ml/1 tbsp capers
15ml/1 tbsp fresh parsley, chopped

Chopping the chilli

1. Cook the spaghetti as directed on the packet.
2. Meanwhile, melt the butter and gently fry the garlic, anchovy and chilli for 1 minute. Stir in the remaining ingredients and simmer gently whilst the pasta cooks.

STEP 2

STEP 2

3. Drain the spaghetti and toss through the hot sauce.

Cook's Notes

TIME: Preparation takes 10 minutes, cooking takes 10 minutes.

VARIATION: Replace the anchovies with chopped prawns.

COOK'S TIP: To prevent irritation, wear a plastic bag over your hand when chopping the chilli.

INSALATA DI MACCHERONI

(Macaroni Salad)
SERVES 4 as a starter

This attractive, brightly coloured pasta salad is ideal for summer buffets and barbecues.

1 yellow pepper
225g/8oz tomatoes, and chopped
6 anchovy fillets, chopped
1 clove garlic, crushed
2.5cm/1-inch piece chilli, seeded and finely chopped
55ml/2 fl oz olive oil
150g/6oz **Buitoni** Maccheroni
Salt and freshly ground pepper
15ml/1 tbsp fresh parsley, chopped

1. Cut the pepper in half and flatten with the palm of your hand.

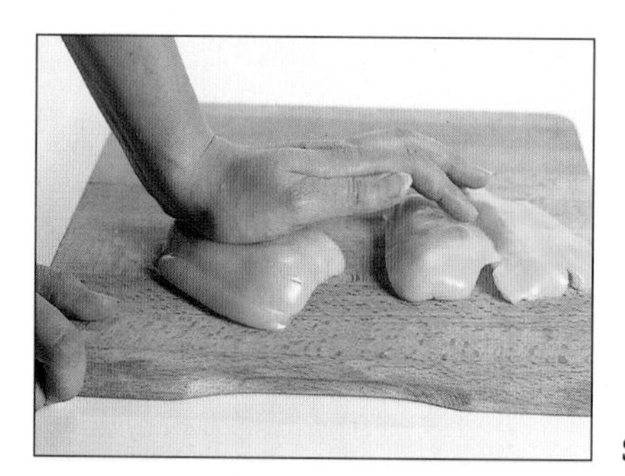

STEP 1

2. Brush the pepper halves with oil and place under a hot grill until charred. Peel off the charred skin and chop the flesh.

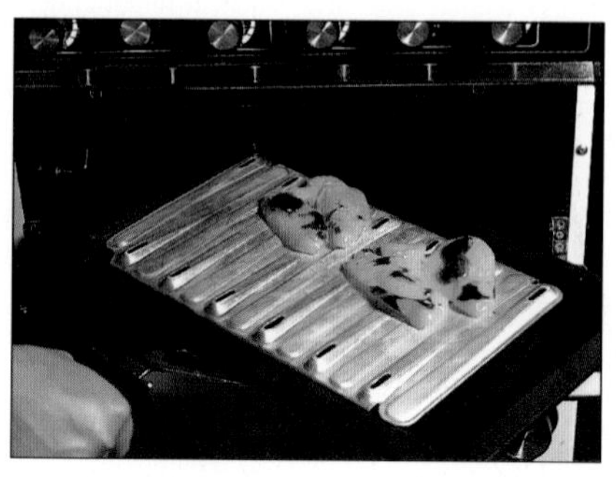

STEP 2

3. Mix together the chopped pepper, tomatoes, anchovies, garlic, chilli and oil.

4. Cook the pasta as directed on the packet. Drain well, then add to the other ingredients.

STEP 4

5. Season to taste, mix well and allow to cool. Sprinkle with parsley and serve.

Cook's Notes

TIME: Preparation takes 15 minutes, cooking takes 15-20 minutes.

VARIATION: Omit the anchovy fillets and replace with 6 black olives, pitted and halved.

COOK'S TIP: After grilling the pepper, wrap it in a teacloth for 10 minutes to help the peel to loosen.

POLLO IN SALSA DI UOVA E LIMONE

(Chicken in Egg and Lemon Sauce)
SERVES 4

This unusual dish has a delicious sauce which complements the chicken perfectly.

4 chicken portions, skinned
Rind of 1 lemon, grated
1 small onion, thinly sliced
550ml/1 pint chicken stock
25g/1oz butter
25g/1oz flour
285ml/½ pint milk
2 egg yolks
30ml/2 tbsps fresh parsley, chopped
30ml/2 tbsps lemon juice
Salt and freshly ground pepper
350g/12oz **Buitoni** Eliche Tricolore
Parsley sprigs and strips of lemon to garnish

1. Place the chicken portions, lemon rind, onion and stock in a pan. Cover and simmer for 45 minutes or until tender. Remove chicken pieces and keep warm.

STEP 1

2. Strain the cooking liquor, melt the butter in a separate pan, blend in the flour and cook for 1 minute.

3. Gradually add the milk and 285ml/½ pint of the cooking liquor. Bring to the boil and cook for 2 minutes.

4. Remove from the heat, and add the egg yolks, parsley, lemon juice and seasoning to taste. Heat gently, but do not boil.

STEP 4

5. Cook the pasta as directed on the packet. Drain, mix half of the sauce with pasta and arrange on a warm serving dish with the cooked chicken. Spoon the rest of the sauce over the chicken and serve garnished with the strips of lemon rind and the parsley.

Cook's Notes

TIME: Preparation takes 10 minutes, cooking takes 50-60 minutes.

SERVING IDEAS: Serve with a selection of green vegetables that have been lightly cooked and tossed in melted butter.

COOK'S TIP: Freeze the remaining cooking liquor for up to three months and use for recipes requiring chicken stock.

CONCHIGLIE CON SALSA DI GORGONZOLA

(Pasta Shells with Gorgonzola Sauce)
SERVES 4

Gorgonzola and bacon provide the flavour in this rich and saucy pasta dish.

350g/12oz **Buitoni** Conchiglie
15ml/1 tbsp olive oil
2 lean rashers of bacon, chopped
1 clove garlic, crushed
285ml/½ pint single cream
150g/6oz Gorgonzola, cubed
Salt and freshly ground pepper
Watercress sprigs to garnish

STEP 2

1. Cook the pasta as directed on the packet.

2. Meanwhile, heat the oil and fry the bacon for 3 minutes. Add the remaining ingredients and heat through very gently.

3. Drain the pasta and toss through the hot sauce. Serve immediately garnished with watercress.

STEP 2

STEP 3

Cook's Notes

TIME: Preparation takes 5 minutes, cooking takes 10-15 minutes.

SERVING IDEAS: Serve with a crisp, crunchy salad selection.

COOK'S TIP: For a milder taste try substituting Dolcelatte for the Gorgonzola.

TORTIGLIONI ALLA ROMAGNOLA

(Tortiglioni with Sausage and Tomato Sauce)
SERVES 4

Surprise your guests with this hot and spicy Italian dish.

225g/8oz **Buitoni** Tortiglioni
15ml 1 tbsp olive oil
1 clove garlic, crushed
1 small onion, chopped
1 small green chilli, finely chopped
225g/8oz Italian salami, skinned and sliced
1 red pepper, deseeded and sliced
350g/12oz tomatoes, skinned and chopped
15ml/1 tbsp fresh parsley, chopped
5ml/1 tsp fresh thyme, chopped
15ml/1 tbsp **Buitoni** tomato purée
45ml/3 tbsps vermouth
Salt and freshly ground black pepper

1. Cook the pasta as directed on the packet.

2. Meanwhile, heat the oil in a large pan and fry the garlic, onion and chilli for 1-2 minutes until lightly browned.

STEP 2

3. Add the sausage and pepper and cook for a further 2-3 minutes. Add the remaining ingredients and simmer gently for 10-12 minutes.

STEP 3

4. Drain the pasta and add to the sauce. Stir well and serve immediately.

STEP 4

Cook's Notes

TIME: Preparation takes 15-20 minutes, cooking takes 25 minutes.

SERVING IDEA: Serve with garlic bread and a tomato salad.

COOK'S TIP: To skin tomatoes, cut a cross in the top of each tomato and plunge into boiling water for 30 seconds, drain in cold water and then peel.

CAPELLI D'ANGELO CON PROSCIUTTO E FUNGHI

(Angel's Hair Pasta with Ham and Mushrooms)
SERVES 4

This lovely, quick pasta dish is suitable for any occasion.

75g/3oz button mushrooms, sliced
15g/½oz butter
75g/3oz cooked smoked ham, thinly sliced and chopped
285ml/½ pint single cream
Salt and freshly ground pepper
250g/9oz **Buitoni** Capelli d'Angelo
Parsley sprigs to garnish

1. Gently sauté the mushrooms in the butter until tender.

STEP 1

2. Add the ham and cream and cook gently, without boiling, until the sauce thickens. Season to taste.

STEP 2

3. Meanwhile, cook the pasta as directed on the packet. Drain and then toss in the hot sauce. Serve garnished with parsley.

STEP 3

Cook's Notes

TIME: Preparation takes 15-20 minutes, cooking takes 30 minutes.

VARIATION: Add a tablespoon of creamed horseradish to the sauce.

COOK'S TIP: Ham bought off the bone has a much better flavour than pre-packed, sliced ham.

ONDULE CON FEGATINI DI POLLO

(Egg Pasta with Chicken Livers)
SERVES 4-6

*Ondule is a premium egg pasta from the **Buitoni Le Preziose** range.*

½ onion, finely chopped
1 clove garlic, crushed
50g/2oz smoked bacon, diced
3 courgettes, sliced
30ml/2 tbsps olive oil
250g/9oz **Buitoni Le Preziose** Ondule
50g/2oz walnut halves
1 sprig mint, chopped
100g/4oz chicken livers, cleaned
55ml/2 fl oz Marsala wine or sweet sherry
140ml/¼ pint double cream
Salt and freshly ground black pepper to taste
Sprigs of mint to garnish

1. Lightly fry onion, garlic, bacon and courgettes in the olive oil for 2-3 minutes.

STEP 1

2. Cook the pasta as directed on the packet.

3. Add the walnuts, mint, chicken livers and Marsala to the courgette mixture and cook on a high heat for 2-3 minutes, stirring constantly until the livers are cooked.

STEP 3

4. Drain pasta. Add cream to liver mixture and heat through. Mix sauce into pasta and serve garnished with mint.

STEP 4

Cook's Notes

TIME: Preparation takes 10 minutes, cooking takes 20 minutes.

SERVING IDEA: Serve with mange tout or sugar snap peas.

COOK'S TIP: Slice the courgettes diagonally to give a more attractive result.

CHIOCCIOLE CON SALMONE E MELANZANE

(Egg Pasta with Salmon and Aubergines)
SERVES 4

*Chiocciole is a snail-shaped egg pasta from the **Buitoni Le Preziose** range.*

½ onion, chopped
1 large aubergine, diced
55ml/2 fl oz olive oil
50g/2oz black olives, pitted
2 tomatoes, skinned, deseeded and sliced
115ml/4 fl oz dry white wine
250g/9oz **Buitoni Le Preziose** Chiocciole
250g/9oz fresh salmon, boned, skinned and roughly chopped
Salt and freshly ground pepper to taste
140ml/¼ pint double cream
Fresh dill sprigs to garnish

1. Lightly fry the onion and aubergine in olive oil for 2-3 minutes. Add black olives, tomatoes and white wine and cook for 3-4 minutes.

STEP 1

2. Meanwhile, cook the pasta as directed on the packet.

3. Add salmon to the aubergine mixture, stir carefully, season and lightly cook for 4 minutes. Add cream and cook for a further 1-2 minutes.

4. Drain pasta, mix with the sauce, sprinkle with the sprigs of dill and serve.

STEP 1

STEP 4

Cook's Notes

TIME: Preparation takes 15-20 minutes, cooking takes 15 minutes.

SERVING IDEA: Serve with dwarf beans or mange tout peas.

COOK'S TIP: To remove the bitterness from the aubergine, place the diced aubergine in a bowl and sprinkle with salt. Leave for 30 minutes, then rinse thoroughly in cold water.

TORCHIETTI STRASCINATI

(Egg Pasta with Sausage and Cream)
SERVES 4-6

Torchietti are shaped like torches and are from the ***Buitoni Le Preziose*** *range.*

250g/9oz **Buitoni Le Preziose** Torchietti
275g/10oz Italian sausage, chopped
15ml/1 tbsp olive oil
½ fennel bulb, chopped
140ml/¼ pint beef stock
2 eggs, beaten
100g/4oz freshly grated Parmesan cheese
140ml/¼ pint double cream
Salt and freshly ground pepper to taste
15ml/1 tbsp parsley, chopped

1. Cook the pasta as directed on the packet. Halfway through cooking the pasta, begin preparing the rest of the ingredients.

2. Lightly fry the sausage in olive oil for 3-4 minutes, add the fennel and cook for a further 2-3 minutes.

STEP 2

3. Drain the pasta and return it to the saucepan.

4. Add the beef stock to the sausage mixture and add this to the drained pasta. Cook for 2-3 minutes.

STEP 4

5. Mix the eggs, Parmesan and cream together and slowly add this to the pasta.

STEP 5

6. Remove from heat, season and pour into a warmed bowl. Sprinkle with parsley and serve.

Cook's Notes

TIME: Preparation takes 10 minutes, cooking takes 20 minutes.

VARIATION: Replace the sausage with 225g/8oz smoked ham or bacon.

COOK'S TIP: The egg, cream and cheese mixture will cook from the heat of the sausage and pasta so do not be tempted to raise the heat or the mixture will curdle.

RICCIOLI AI FRUTTI DI MARE

(Egg Pasta with Seafood)
SERVES 4

This impressive dish is perfect fare for a dinner party or a special celebration meal.

30ml/2 tbsps olive oil
2 scallops, sliced
25g/1oz shelled prawns
25g/1oz shelled mussels
12 clams, shelled
12 asparagus tips
1 sprig of basil, chopped
Juice of ½ lemon
Salt and freshly ground black pepper
250g/9oz **Buitoni Le Preziose** Riccioli
55ml/2 fl oz white wine
5ml/1 tsp **Buitoni** tomato purée
400g/14oz can chopped tomatoes
25g/1oz butter
Parmesan cheese (to serve)

1. Heat the olive oil and lightly fry the shellfish for 2-3 minutes. Add the asparagus tips, basil and lemon juice, season lightly and cook for 3-4 minutes.

STEP 1

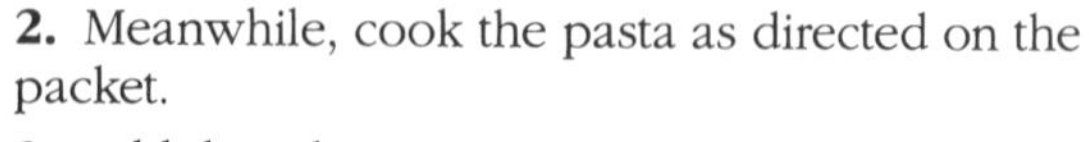

2. Meanwhile, cook the pasta as directed on the packet.

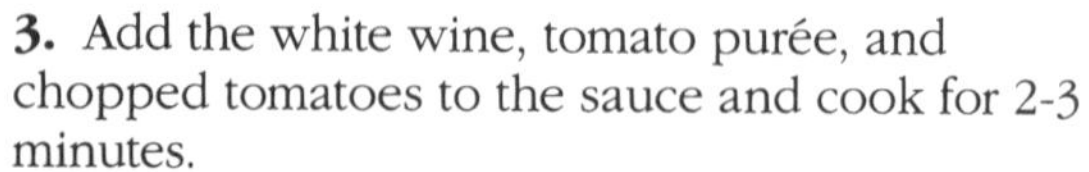

3. Add the white wine, tomato purée, and chopped tomatoes to the sauce and cook for 2-3 minutes.

STEP 3

4. Drain the pasta and fry in the butter for 1-2 minutes. Add the pasta to the sauce, pour into warm bowls and sprinkle with Parmesan cheese.

STEP 4

Cook's Notes

TIME: Preparation takes 15 minutes, cooking takes 15-20 minutes.

SERVING IDEA: Serve with lime wedges and garnish with an unshelled king prawn.

VARIATION: Use any combination of your favourite shellfish such as crab or lobster.

COOK'S TIP: If fresh asparagus is not available, use the canned variety.

INDEX

Photography by Peter Barry
Recipes Prepared and Styled by Helen Burdett
Designed by Judith Chant
Edited by Jillian Stewart